OUR NATIONAL FINANCES

LETTER

OF

HON. ROBT. J. WALKER

EX-SECRETARY OF THE TREASURY.

Chronicle Print, Washington, D. C.

LETTER OF HON. R. J. WALKER.

WASHINGTON CITY, November 30, 1867.

To the People of the United States:

The great question of maintaining the public faith now agitates the nation, and engages the attention of Congress. Inseparably connected with this question is the revisal of our bank and currency and revenue systems. Whatever concerns the public faith touches all the great interests of the country. It deeply affects the revenue of the Government, as well as the wages of labor and the income and business of the people. No American requires any apology for discussing these great questions. My own individual connection with them was constant and earnest, from the commencement to the close of the rebellion, and I feel that my position is one involving great responsibilities: Our national banking law, after its rejection by Congress, was finally adopted on the publication of an elaborate essay written by me, at the request of the Secretary of the Treasury. Subsequently, at his request, when he found it necessary to bring gold or its equivalent here from Europe to sustain our credit, I repaired there, remaining nearly two years, as the financial agent of the Government. I published there numerous essays, over my signature, showing the wealth and resources of our country, and how untarnished was our national faith and honor. These essays, in English, French, and German, were sent to all the European bankers, through whose advice investments are made. They represented the certainty of the punctual payment of the *principal* and *interest* of our Five-twenty six per cent. loans in *gold*. I went to Europe under the appointment of Mr. Chase, but with letters also from Mr. Lincoln and Mr. Seward. So bitter then was the hostility of Louis Napoleon and the late Lord Palmerston to this country, that, whilst the so-called confederate loan had nearly reached in Europe par in gold, our United States stocks could find no place on the London or Paris exchange, and our cause no hearing in the leading press of either city. We had many friends in the British Cabinet, but it was then that Lord Palmerston and his life-long friend, Louis Napoleon, were engaged in a conspiracy to drive republicanism from the face of the earth. It was then that dazzling visions of dukedoms, if not of diadems, were glittering before the eyes of many a confederate leader. It was then that Napoleon was spreading the imperial purple over the halls of the Montezumas, and appealing to the Latin race of America to unfurl the banner of the European dynastic system. It was then that British cruisers (miscalled Confederate) were burning our ships and cargoes, and driving our commerce from the ocean. It was then that the English Premier was preparing for Prince Alfred a throne in British America, now dwindled into the hybrid, discordant, temporary Dominion of Canada. It was then, at the period of our deepest gloom and danger, that a still small voice was heard in our favor from Holland, where Franklin had negotiated our first loan. It was then that the still louder notes of hope and sympathy fell like music upon my ears from the great German Fatherland. I visited both countries, unheralded and unknown, in 1863. Satisfied that any public call for a loan would be defeated by the machinations of France and England, I never announced my official capacity, nor asked for any American loan. I published my financial essays over my own name, merely as an American citizen, exhibiting the vast resources, the wonderful progress of our country, and the certainty of our success in crushing the rebellion. These essays were sent by thousands to all the principal bankers of Europe. In a few months I visited again nearly every city of Holland and Germany, giving me an opportunity to discuss the question personally with these bankers, and enforce the written arguments already made. The result was that in a brief period the *people of Germany*, emphatically the *great masses of the people*, took several hundred millions of our loan at the same rates as our own citizens. Let it be remembered that this was a period of great apprehension as to the result of our contest, and that the credit of our greenbacks rested mainly on these bonds, in which they could be funded, and that the demand for them in Germany, as well as here, to organize the national banks, prevented our currency from disappearing in the gathering mists of depreciation. Our greatest peril was financial, and although the glorious deeds of our army and navy, and their gallant leaders, saved us on the ocean and the land, yet the Secretary of the Treasury was the real generalissimo of the contest. These German and other loans, based upon these United States five-twenties, constituted, to a vast extent, the *price we agreed to pay* to enable us to maintain the Government and preserve the Union. And now, shall we hesitate about the full payment of such loans as these? But, especially, can I, on whose representation so many hundred millions of these loans were taken, now, whilst the great issues are being discussed, and soon to be decided, without a burning sense of shame and dishonor, remain longer silent?

The question to be discused is very comprehensive, and requires a review of our whole system of loans and banks and currency, as well as revenue and taxation.

We have now a depreciated paper currency called legal tenders, amounting, according to the returns on the 1st of November, to three hundred and eighty-seven million eight hundred and seventy-one thousand four hundred and seventy-seven dollars, ($387,871,477.) We had, also, then, in the Treasury, one hundred and eleven millions five hundred and forty thousand three hundred and seventeen dollars (111,540,317) in coin, and twenty-two millions four hundred and fifty-eight thousand and eighty dollars ($22,458,080) in currency, making one hundred and thirty-three million nine hundred and ninety-eight thousand three hundred and ninety-seven dollars ($133,998,397) in all. Deducting this from the above, leaves two hundred and fifty-three million eight hundred and seventy-three thousand and eighty dollars, ($253,873,080.) It may be assumed, then, that a loan of two hundred and fifty millions of dollars in gold, together with the balance now in the Treasury, would redeem all our legal tenders, and restore immediately a specie currency. The question is, how, or where, and in what manner, and at what rate this loan can be effected. As a general rule I am opposed to foreign loans, and made none such while Secretary of the Treasury, even to carry on our war with Mexico. But the loans then required were very small as compared with the amount now to be obtained. We did not suspend specie payments, and the condition of the country was very different then. The object now is to resume specie payments, and should we now borrow $250,000,000 in gold at home, even if it could be obtained, the rates would be most extravagant, and the loan would so exhaust the available moneyed resources of the country as to cause a great and immediate contraction of the currency, to be followed by a terrible revulsion. No, this must be a *foreign* loan, so as to bring the gold here to create an expansion, not in paper, but in specie, and to infuse new life-blood into all the channels of industry. It is contraction, without resumption, that is driving the country to the verge of repudiation, and threatening most disastrous consequences to the honor and interests of the nation. The rules which often force banks to contract have no bearing upon the operations of the Government at this time. So far as the value of our legal-tenders is concerned, we are much more remote from resumption than we were when the war closed. No one thought of repudiation then, but the idea has become widely diffused, growing exclusively out of a forced, artificial, and unnecessary contraction of the currency, connected with a most oppressive and intolerable system of taxation. I say the contraction was and is forced and unnecessary, because we could, by a foreign loan, then have resumed specie payments; and, with a proper change in our revenue system, and the restoration of the Union, now be in a condition of unbounded prosperity. No one, before this, has ever threatened to stain the faith and honor of the nation, and but for this system of contraction and taxation the spectral shade of repudiation would never have been evoked from the dark abyss of infamy and crime. Contraction is only advocated with a view to ultimate resumption of specie payments. But why contract, and thus depress all our industry, when we can immediately resume without contraction? If we are not to resume until the whole paper currency is gradually taken in, how many years will it take to accomplish it? What will be the condition of the country in the meantime, whilst the contraction is constantly going on? And what will it be when all our legal-tenders shall have been thus exhausted, together with the national bank currency based upon them? Why, our condition would be growing worse and worse every day, and at the close we would be left almost without any currency whatever. Why should our people be thus oppressed and racked and tortured by a forced contraction of the currency, which is the life-blood of all our industry. Why this constant drainage of all the veins and arteries of our industrial system? Do we want bleeding now, and do we want it continued from month to month, and from year to year, until we shall have exhausted the system by this Saugrado policy? But there are two kinds of contraction—the one by the gradual exhaustion of our paper currency, and the other by a domestic loan, draining from the people all the available money of the country.

I, then, am for a foreign loan, so as at once to supply the vacuum, to replenish our exhausted resources, and resume specie payments, with all its incalculable benefits to our faith, our credit, and our industry.

What real objection is there to a foreign loan? Did Washington and the patriots of

'76 object to it when Franklin negotiated our first foreign loan in Holland? Did not Mr. Lincoln, concurring with Mr. Chase, warmly advocate it, when we thus obtained the necessary money to replenish an exhausted treasury during the late rebellion?

It is certain, on resumption, that this whole loan would be taken by the masses of the people of Germany at par, or higher, in gold for six per cent. bonds. We borrowed $250,000,000 from the Germans in 1863-4 to carry on the war then. And I would open the new foreign loan at Hamburg, Berlin, and Frankfort, aided by Count Bismarck, who is as great a friend of American as he is of German unity. We should not go to London or Paris, from whose Bourse and Exchange we were driven in 1863-4; but to the *people* of Germany, who, at that period, took several hundred millions of our bonds, all of which would rise to par upon the success of our new loan and the resumption of specie payments. Not a few of the German people who took this new loan would emigrate and join their countrymen here, felling the forests and cultivating our prairies, enlarging our wealth, diminishing our taxes, and carrying freedom and civilization over our continent, from the rising to the setting sun. I would print these bonds in German and English, as a compliment to the German people, who came to our rescue in 1863 and 1864. They should be payable in German coins, with their equivalents noted; their offer should be accompanied with our resumption of specie payments, and the statistics of our wealth and progress, with copies of our homestead law, and a full description of our magnificent public domain.

Let us do this, and we can obtain the whole six per cent. loan at or above par in Germany, and the golden current will rush Westward, replenishing the channels of industry with a specie currency, reviving our drooping business, and demolishing the gold board and gold gambling in the only practicable way, namely, by an immediate resumption of specie payments. But if we do not now resume, and whilst the repudiation question is hanging over us undecided, we attempt a loan at home or abroad, it will either be an entire failure, or the rates will be so ruinous as to exhaust the substance of the people. Strange that we—a country with a large debt—have not fully realized the immense importance of our national credit. With such a nation, credit is wealth, credit is capital; and so fully has this been established in England, that, whilst their three per cent. consols are 94 in gold, our six per cents. are at 70, thus compelling us to pay an interest very nearly three times as great as England. And yet, at the relative rate of progress, as shown by the census of both countries, (that of England being 37 per cent. in each decade, and ours 126.45 per cent.,) our wealth, in 1901, would be largely more than quadruple that of England. If the English credit was no better than ours, they would never pay the principal or interest of their public debt. There is no reason for this difference except this, that if any member of the British Parliament should propose, by evasion or otherwise, to repudiate the principal or interest of their public debt, he would be instantly expelled from his seat in the House of Commons, and because their system of finance is based upon acknowledged rules of political economy. National credit is a part of the national wealth, especially with a nation in debt, or one ever likely to be in debt, or engaged in war, and, in maintaining the credit of the nation, we not only sustain its honor, but we diminish the interest upon its public debt, with a corresponding decrease of taxation. Whilst contraction, as we have seen, is death by a slow and lingering process, expansion of depreciated paper is immediate financial suicide. If we cannot resume by contraction, when our depreciated Government currency is less than $400,000,000, how can we ever accomplish the object, when, as proposed by some, it shall reach $2,000,000,000, accompanied by evasive and disgraceful repudiation. The only remedy is immediate resumption, to be accomplished by a foreign loan. In this way we can at once make our legal tenders and bank currency based upon them equivalent to specie, and raise our bonds at home and abroad at least to par in gold. This would make an immediate difference (as will be shown hereafter) in the active wealth of the country (its circulation and negotiable credits) of more than one billion of dollars. Such an enormous and immediate increase of our active wealth, accompanied by all its invigorating influences upon every industrial pursuit, would cause the country to rise at once from its depression, and commence a new career of prosperity and progress.

I have said we should authorize an immediate foreign loan of $250,000,000; but, perhaps, not half of it would be required. We can effect the loan for the whole amount, if needed, so as to give us the immediate potentiality of resumption; but we need only draw for it as it is wanted, receiving the benefits of the exchange, and allowing interest only upon the sums actually paid upon our drafts at maturity. After consultation with the bankers of Europe, immediately preceding my return here, I made this suggestion to Mr. Fessenden, then Secretary of the Treasury, in December, 1864. Although opposed, generally, to foreign loans,

I think he thought favorably of it, especially when peace should be restored; but, as he was about to retire from the Treasury, nothing was done at that time. Mr. Chase, also, gave the suggestion of resumption his cordial approval. It was as clear to me then as it is now that unless we adopted this policy we must go into contraction or expansion of a depreciated currency, each leading to repudiation and ruin. Our greenbacks then were much depreciated, yet, upon a safe deposit of our bonds as collateral, we could then have got the gold at the rate of six per cent. per annum, and immediately have resumed specie payments. I feel confident that, upon resumption now, we can get the whole amount in gold at a rate not exceeding six per cent. The European bankers have now studied our statistics, and they understand our boundless resources. All we want is to sustain and improve our national credit, to put an end to an irredeemable and depreciated paper currency, and scout indignantly repudiation in all its forms, whether direct or evasive. British consols, bearing three per cent. interest per annum, as we have seen, bring 94 in gold, whilst our six per cents. are at 70. Yet, as shown in the third edition of my financial London letters of 1863–'4, the following were the actual statistics from the census of England and America:

Our national wealth in 1850 was..$7,135,780,228
" " " 1860 " 16,159,616,068
England's national wealth in 1861..................................31,500,000,000

United States increase from 1850 to 1860, 126 45-100 per cent.

England's increase from 1851 to 1861, 37 per cent.

Assuming these ratios, the wealth of the United Kingdom would increase as follows:

1861	$31,500,000,000
1871	43,155,000,000
1881	59,122,350,000
1891	80,997,619,500
1901	110,966,837,715

And that of the United States as follows:

1860	$16,159,616,068
1870	36,593,450,585
1880	82,865,868,849
1890	187,314,353,225
1900	423,330,438,288
1910	465,663,482,116

Thus our wealth in thirty-three years would be more than quadruple that of England.

The European bankers, and especially the people of Germany, now fully understand these results. They know, also, the reasons of our hitherto wonderful progress—our free institutions, our immense emigration, adding nearly three thousand millions to our wealth from 1850 to 1860, and our magnificent public domain, with our homestead and pre-emption systems. They know, also, our capacity for resumption, and look with amazement and distrust at our failure to do so.

I am opposed to any considerable payments *at present* in extinguishment of the principal of our public debt; not because I regard a public debt a blessing; far otherwise; but when the debt is incurred the great question is, by what system and at what rate of payment will the public interest be best promoted.

To decrease the principal of our public debt by present annual payments of fifty to one hundred millions of dollars is to increase to that extent the present burden of taxation, which is grinding out the substance of our people and immensely retarding the progress of our wealth. That it is vastly injurious now will not be denied, nor will posterity thank us for it. We have seen that at the rate of progress from 1850 to 1860 our wealth in 1901 would be $465,663,832,116. Now suppose that we should at that date, by this oppressive process, have extinguished our whole national debt of $2,500,000,000. According to every principle of political economy, such a process, so oppressive to our industry and retarding so much the progress of our wealth, would have diminished the aggregate in 1901 at least ten per cent. It would be much greater, but even at ten per cent. the diminution in 1901 would be $46,566,348,211. Now, deduct from this the whole debt then extinguished, and the difference would exhibit a loss of national wealth in 1901 exceeding $44,000,000,000 as the result of such oppressive taxation. Now to pay six per cent. interest annually and reduce the principal of such a debt as ours more than $500,000,000 in thirty-two years is more than England or any other country has ever been able to accomplish in the same time. To do this would require an annual payment (exclusive of the interest) of over $16,000,000 a year. But our payments ought to commence with a much smaller sum, say beginning with only $1,000,000, and go on increasing at the rate of $1,000,000 a year, making the second payment $2,000,000, the third $3,000,000, and the last $32,000,000 in 1900; and besides meeting the annual interest, we should have paid more than $500,000,000 of the principal of the public debt in 1900. Thus we would pay annually in *proportion* to our constantly increasing *means*; for we must reflect that according to the census we could pay $29,000,000 as easily in proportion to our wealth in 1900 as we could $1,000,000 in 1860.

Those, generally, who oppose contraction or resumption, favor what they call expansion, and many of them would pay off our whole Five-twenty loan in greenbacks. Now, this, with our present greenbacks, and the convertible Seven-thirties, would make a total greenback currency of nearly *two billions* of dollars, and, with the national bank currency, redeemable in greenbacks, nearly twenty-three hundred millions of currency, mere naked promises of payment, fundable in none of the stocks of the Government. Now, our present currency, bank and legal tenders, is worth in gold nearly $500,000,000. Would the expanded currency be worth that much? I think its first value would be much less, and that it would go on constantly diminishing in value until it would, in no brief period, share the fate of French assignats and continental money. There would be a nominal, but no real available expansion of the currency; for the increased amount would purchase less than the smaller, but far more valuable, circulation. Such a system would, in fact, be depreciation only—a vast addition to the volume of the currency, but a diminution of its aggregate value. Such a currency would not be worth at the start twenty cents on the dollar in gold. The first result would be to increase the expenses of the Government and of living nearly four-fold, with no corresponding increase of wages or of revenue. The expenses of the Government, paid in this depreciated paper, would swell to nearly two billions a year, and the excess of our annual expenditures over receipts would exceed a billion of dollars a year, swelling yearly, with the necessary demand for a further inflation, until the whole mass would become worthless, and leave the Government and people without money or credit.

The inflation of an irredeemable paper currency necessarily leads to depreciation, and can end only in repudiation and bankruptcy. How can it be otherwise? How can we contract when there are no bonds in which the currency can be funded, or bonds the value of which has been destroyed by the action of the Government. And if contraction is grievous when our currency is five or six hundred millions, how infinitely more oppressive will contraction become when the currency is increased to one or two billions of dollars. But let us see what the effect of this depreciation would be on present values. Our national bank notes and legal-tenders amount to near $700,000,000, now worth about $500,000,000 in gold to those who hold them. The gold value of this money, at twenty cents on the dollar in gold, would be only $140,000,000, thus annihilating at a blow values to the extent of $360,000,000. This reduction of values is in the *money*, the *only money* held by the people of the United States. This would reduce hundreds of thousands to want and bankruptcy. It would convulse and demoralize the whole country, and cause the pillars of the Government to rock upon their bases. But the annihilation of values would not be confined to the *money* of the people, but would extend to our two billions of dollars of bonds, worth now to the holders $1,400,000,000 in gold. But by the depreciation process these bonds, or their substitute in currency, would not exceed twenty cents on the dollar in gold, or $400,000,000. Here is a loss of one billion of dollars, which, added to the loss on currency, annihilates values to the extent of $1,360,000,000 in gold, or its equivalent. Recollect that the values thus annihilated constitute the *active* capital, the *money*, and *negotiable* credits of the people. Why, the revulsion would be fearful, and the burning lava of a nation's wrath would roll over the authors of the dread catastrophe.

But what of the national honor? What of our proud position among the nations of the earth? And what of the cause of self-government, when we, its bright exemplar and trusted guardian, should have covered the great cause with the mantle of disgrace and shame? The picture may be darkly shadowed, but it is by the pencil of truth. Indeed, no mortal vision can penetrate those dismal caverns, the abodes of want and misery, where would wander, in agony and despair, the wretched victims of a nation's broken faith and tarnished honor. Remember this would be a repudiation, not of our bonds only, but of the *money of the people*, the notes of the national banks, and of the deposits in them, and in the savings banks, all redeemable in greenbacks, and the greenbacks themselves. The working man or woman, who had stored away a few greenbacks for marketing, or fuel, or flour, or groceries, would find their money so depreciated that they could not supply their daily wants. And now as to the wages of labor. Experience and philosophy prove that wages are the last to rise with a depreciated currency, because the children of toil cannot wait, but must work at wages lower in reality, until the great law of supply and demand, gradually but slowly, restores the equilibrium. Indeed, in a vast number of cases, where there are contracts for work by the month, or year, or job, payable in currency, they could be liquidated in an almost worthless paper. The repudiator and inflationist would pay labor in a greatly depreciated currency. The contractionist, after a long and ruinous delay, would pay him eventually in gold. The resumptionist would pay him now, henceforth, and forever, in gold. If there is any principle that is vital, *it is this*, that *the wages of labor should be always payable in gold, or its real equivalent.*

And now, if we inaugurate the reign of a

depreciated paper currency, how many of the toiling millions of Europe will come here to swell our wealth and power? How much foreign capital will come! Nay, let us rather ask, how much and who will remain to encounter the fearful risks and losses flowing from a broken faith and worthless currency? All confidence would vanish; there would be a vast exodus of wealth and labor, a general impoverishment, and a great decline of all values.

We have seen that the loss in the gold values of our bonds and currency would be equal to $1,360,000,000; but the gains between their present values, say $2,500,000,000, in bonds and legal-tenders and national bank notes by a rise to par, would be $840,000,000. Add this to the first sum, and the difference to the country between repudiation and resumption would be $2,200,000,000 in gold. Deduct, (this we should not,) the proposed loan, and we have $1,950,000,000 as the gain by resumption, as compared with depreciation and expansion. But this is far from all the benefit that would accrue to the people from the resumption policy. If there is any maxim in political economy proved by philosophy and tested by experience, it is that an irredeemable paper currency is a forced loan, exacted as a tax from the people, not in proportion to wealth or property, but bearing with special severity on all industrious pursuits, and imposing the severest burdens on the wages of labor. Such a currency deranges all business by constant fluctuations in prices, renders all calculations unreliable, and all pursuits uncertain. In fact, such a system is almost as perilous as gambling, with prices varying so much, almost every day and hour, changing with the throws of the die in the gold room, or intensified by Government sales of the precious metals, and funding, and other necessary operations of the Treasury connected with the currency, and vitally affecting its value from day to day. As well might we change the weights and measures from day to day, and expect the business of the country to be prosperous and successful, as to accomplish the same purpose by such great and rapid and constant changes in the currency, which are our measures of values. If the yard, the gallon, or the bushel could be changed every day by transactions in the gold room, or by operations of the Treasury, the business of the country would in reality be no more fluctuating and uncertain than it is rendered by similar changes in the values of money. All the benefits of skill and experience derived from years of devotion to business pursuits, are lost through fluctuations in the currency, which no sagacity or skill can anticipate. When we reflect that each nation is but a part of the great community of States, united by ties of commerce, business, and interchanges, and find the rest of the world sustained by a specie currency, which is of uniform, universal international value, how can we, who are dealing with depreciated paper, expect to compete successfully with those countries whose money is gold, or its actual equivalent? No nation has ever tried this experiment without vast sacrifices and great failure. So long as the currency of the world is gold, any nation departing from this standard impairs its own power of successful competition, and gradually drives its products from the markets of the world. It is true that it may, to a certain extent, so far as smuggling does not open the safety-valve, keep out foreign imports for a time, thereby annihilating its exports; but prices soon rise at home in a ratio corresponding with the augmented duties, and, the check becoming ineffectual, is sought to be remedied by augmented tariffs. It is totally impossible for a nation like the United States to withdraw from the business operations of the world, and it is equally impracticable to carry on successful international exchanges when the money of the country is depreciated paper. We see this now in all business and in all the industrial pursuits; and, next to the wages of labor, American manufactures are most injured by a fluctuating and depreciated paper currency. We see, also, that our tonnage is constantly declining, and that our ships and steamers are almost driven from the ocean. From 1846 to 1856 our exports, domestic products, and manufactures were more than tripled, and they ought now, with the increase of our wealth, to have greatly surpassed those of England, and reached nearly a thousand millions of dollars. Where are they now, and to what point are they going? Let the Treasury reports answer the question. For all these evils there is but one remedy, an IMMEDIATE RESUMPTION of specie payments, accompanied by a VAST REDUCTION OF TAXATION.

England exported, last year, products exceeding in value seven hundred millions of dollars. This, with a population at least five millions less than ours, and with far inferior resources. Our exports for the same period scarcely reached half this sum.

In truth, the whole machinery of the business of the country is deranged, and nothing but resumption will restore it to proper action.

In my Texas letter of January, 1844, and in my subsequent Treasury reports from 1845 to 1849, I predicted that New York city, under a proper system, would rapidly advance to the command of the commerce of the world. That prediction was in course of progressive fulfilment, until our gigantic war expenditures forced upon the country the suspension of specie payments, resulting in a depreciated currency and an almost intolerable taxation. Where is she now in the career of progress as compared with London, her great and only rival? Let the account of her tonnage and business tell the story. And yet New York has incalculable advantages over London in such a rivalry. She is, in point of latitude, ten degrees nearer the average products of the earth, according to area, than London, and she represents a continent stretching from ocean to ocean, and not a little island scarcely larger than New York. Even now, on returning to a specie currency, or one in all respects its real equivalent, remove the intolerable burden of taxation, strike the shackles from her commerce and industry, and she will commence a new career, surpassing all her former progress.

The question of commanding the commerce of the world is one of gigantic proportions, affecting not merely the city of New York, but every other American city, and the entire people of the Union. The local jealousies against her are opposing nature and destiny, and are anti-American and absurd; for the real alternative is not between New York and any of our other cities, but between *New York and London alone*. Now, it is ascertained that England, by commanding through London the commerce of the world, increases British wealth to the extent of at least five hundred millions of dollars every year. And this is what we lose by failing to make New York, as we can, the centre of universal commerce. The loss is not to New York alone, but to every American city, and to every State and Territory of the Union. The annual loss to us, in fact, amounts to a sum that, in five years, could pay the whole national debt. Whilst New York by latitude is ten degrees nearer than London, *by area*, to the products of the earth, yet London being nearly in latitude 52, and so small a portion comparatively of the earth's surface north of that parallel being productive, the real gain to New York far exceeds ten degrees. The population and value of products north of New York are very nearly equal to those south, and the ratio constantly augmenting in her favor.

Accompanying the resumption of specie payments, and essential as a part of the system designed to restore the prosperity of the country, must be an immense and immediate reduction of taxation. To accomplish this, we must reduce expenditures, restore the Union, and disburse only the sums required in peace.

Our expenditures, exclusive of the interest on the public debt for the year preceding the war, were $59,848,474, of which the expenditures for the War and Navy Departments were $27,922,917, leaving our other expenditures $31,925,555. Now, supposing these to increase fifty per cent., (which should not be,) it would make them $48,000,000. Now, if we double in time of peace our war and navy expenditures, which is too great an increase, this would make them $56,000,000. This would make our whole annual expenditures, exclusive of the interest on the public debt, $104,000,000. To effect this reduction, we must resume specie payments, for, by paying in gold, the Government *saves at once nearly thirty per cent. of its expenditures.*

The second great reduction should be in the mode of extinguishing the principal of the public debt. These payments, as I have attempted to show, should be graduated in proportion to our means. Beginning with one million dollars per annum, increasing the payment by a like sum every year, and terminating in 1900 with a payment of thirty-two millions of dollars per annum. By thus graduating the payments in proportion to our means, we should lift an immense burden of taxation from the people.

Another item, growing out of the repeal of taxes and excises, amounting to nearly $8,000,000 a year, would be the disbanding of nearly our whole army of tax gatherers and the expenses incident thereto, which, I shall discuss hereafter, when considering the question of taxation. In this way, and by avoiding all unnecessary expenses, we can reduce our expenditures, exclusive of interest on the public debt, to $104,000,000. I have not before me the report of the Secretary of the Treasury for this year, and can therefore only give the expenditures for the year ending the 1st of July, 1866. These, as given by the Secretary, were $387,693,199. This is exclusive of payments on account of principal and interest of the public debt. Now these last payments amount to $140,000,000 a year. This would make our whole expenditures, at a maximum, $244,000,000. This would be a reduction of $143,693,199, and compared with the expenditures of the fiscal year ending the 1st July, 1866, would enable us to reduce to that vast extent the taxes of the people.

This revenue of $244,000,000 a year, as a maximum, I would derive from three sources alone:

1. By a tariff for revenue.
2. By an excise on wines, malt and spirituous liquors, and tobacco; abolishing all other internal taxation.
3. By a tax on our national banks, based upon just and fair equivalents, remembering how essential they are to the prosperity of the country, and that we must not drive them into liquidation by unfair and unequal taxation, and thus revive the wretched State bank system.

A tariff for revenue, as experience has shown, instead of depressing, improves all industrial pursuits, including manufactures, and vastly augments the wealth of the country. Under the tariff of 1846, as shown by the census, our wealth increased from 1850 to 1860, 126 45-100 per cent.; whereas, from 1840 to 1850, the increase was only 64 per cent.; from 1830 to 1840, 42 per cent.; and from 1820 to 1830, 41 per cent. So also, from 1850 to 1860 our agricultural products increased 95 per cent., and our manufactures 87 per cent., being, in both cases, nearly double any preceding ratio of increase. So also, our exports, imports, and revenue nearly tripled in the same period of time, and our domestic trade rose nearly in the same ratio. This augmented ratio is not the result of increase of population, which, from 1850 to 1860, was less than 36 per cent. The Irish famine was supposed by my opponents to account for the increase the first year, although the decreased price paid abroad that year for our cotton nearly equalled the additional sum paid by England for our breadstuffs and provisions. But the *next year* and *the next*, before any gold had reached here from California, our exports and revenue went on augmenting in a corresponding ratio, rising in eight years from $22,000,000, under the tariff of 1842, to $64,000,000 under the tariff of 1846. But, if it were true, that we could thus wonderfully prosper under a revenue tariff after the gold discoveries, why not continue the system? These discoveries, however, produced no effect whatever until after the fiscal year ending on the 30th June, 1849. The truth is, however, even after that date, these wonderful results as to imports, exports, and revenue, must be attributed, in a very slight degree to these gold discoveries, for the following reasons: First, the rate of increase during the first three years of the operation of the tariff of 1846 down to the 30th of June 1849, before any of this gold had reached here, was greater than the rate of increase at any succeeding period. The reason of this greater ratio of increase from 1846 to 1849 was, that when the shackles of our commerce and industry, including the immense indirect taxation imposed by the tariff of 1842, were suddenly removed by the reduced tariff of 1846, the country sprung forward at a bound unprecedented in the history of the world; second, the great political economists of Europe have published, at various periods, and especially in 1863, authentic tables, giving the exact facts, from the prices current of all articles throughout the world, during the several years since the gold discoveries. These tables show that the additional prices caused by these gold discoveries amounted to about one per centum per annum. It is true that a contrary opinion had prevailed to a considerable extent, based, not upon facts, but upon certain conjectural theories of prices and currency. The ideas of these theorists (now abandoned) were that prices would increase in a proportion equal to the additional gold produced. But they ignored several important facts: First. How very small a part specie performs in carrying on international exchanges, and even domestic business. Second. The great fact that in a series of years the value of gold, like that of all other articles, is mainly regulated by the law of supply and demand. Thus, if an increase of gold should so stimulate industry and new enterprises as to make the augmented demand equal to the increased supply, prices would remain unchanged. This is now the conceded law as to the precious metals. A further conclusive proof as to the existence of this law is furnished by our own census tables of 1850 and 1860. Thus, the great increase of our wealth, and of our products, over all other decades, is attributed to the gold discoveries; but although these might increase *values*, they would not increase *quantities*. By looking at table No. 36, in the preliminary report on the eighth census, (pages 198 to 210, including the *additional* returns on these pages,) the following will be found to be the results, as to agricultural products, from 1850 to 1860:

	1850.	1860.
Horses, (number)..........	4,336,719	7,303,972
Asses and mules...........	559,391	1,396,339
Milch cows, working oxen, and other cattle.........	18,378,857	28,987,346
Sheep......................	21,723,220	24,823,371
Swine......................	30,354,213	36,023,472
Wheat, (bushels)..........	100,485,944	171,183,381
Rye, (bushels)............	14,188,813	20,976,286
Indian corn, (bushels).....	592,071,104	830,451,707
Oats, (bushels)............	146,584,179	172,554,688
Tobacco, (lbs.)............	199,758,655	429,390,771
Ginned cotton, (bales)....	2,445,793	5,198,077
Wool, (lbs.)...............	52,516,959	60,511,343
Peas and beans, (bushels).	9,219,901	15,188,013
Irish potatoes, (bushels)..	65,797,896	110,571,201
Sweet do. do ..	38,268,148	41,606,302
Barley, (bushels)..........	5,167,015	15,635,119
Buckwheat, (bushels).....	8,956,912	17,664,914
Wine, (gallons)...........	221,249	1,860,008
Butter, (lbs.).............	313,345,306	460,509,854
Hay, (tons)...............	13,838,642	19,129,128
Clover seed, (bushels).....	468,978	929,010
Grass seed, (bushels)......	416,831	900,386
Hemp, (tons)..............	34,871	104,490
Hops, (lbs.)...............	3,497,029	11,010,012
Maple sugar, (lbs.)........	34,253,436	38,863,884
Cane sugar, (hhds.).......	237,133	302,205
Molasses, (gallons).......	12,700,991	25,517,699
Beeswax and honey, (lbs.).	14,853,128	26,386,855

Rice, (lbs.)—small decrease.
Cheese—slight increase.
Flax—large decrease.
Flaxseed—small increase.
Silk cocoons—decrease of 4,281 pounds.

When we remember now that the increase of our agricultural products from 1850 to 1860 was ninety-five per cent., the table I have given, as to quantities and numbers, shows an increase fully equal to eighty-five per cent., thus leaving about one per cent. per annum for the effect of gold in increasing values, thus verifying the tables of the European economists. As to manufactures, values only are given, and not the comparative quantities; but by table No. 132, page 129 of the compendium of the census of 1850, it will be found that the number of persons employed in manufacturing establishments that year was 944,991, while page 59 of the census of 1860 gives the number for that year as 1,385,000. Thus, whilst the increased numbers of persons employed in manufacturing in 1860 as compared with 1850 was not quite fifty per cent., yet the vast discoveries and improvements in machinery as applied to manufactures during that period must have increased the product at least twenty-five per cent., as compared with the same number of workmen, thus again demonstrating that very little more than ten per cent. was due to the increased value of manufactures in 1860 as compared with 1850, growing out of the gold discoveries. Whatever may be the exact per centage of increase caused by these discoveries, it could not in any way have effected the results from 1846 to 1849, and from 1850 to 1860 the increased value produced in this way could very little have exceeded ten per cent. All candid men, who are searching after truth, must attribute the wonderful success of the tariff of 1846, as to imports, exports, and revenue, to causes almost wholly unconnected with the gold discoveries. On a question like this, where our present system of taxation is so intolerable, and so much wisdom and patriotism are required to avoid most disastrous consequences, should we not all discard previous prepossessions and prejudices, and search for the truth, wherever it may lead us? And here, may I not ask, among the thousands of articles that are made and consumed by man, nearly all of which come under the operations of our tariff, is it reasonable to suppose that if one set of men take up all these articles separately, as was done in framing the tariff of 1846, so as to ascertain what duty on each article will bring the greatest revenue, and another set in whole, or in part, discard the principle, is it not clear that those who impose the duties with a view to revenue will produce a much greater result than those who look mainly to what is called protection?

But there was another reason why the tariff of 1846 so soon tripled our revenue; and that was the mode of collecting the duties. The tables annexed to the Treasury reports of 1846–7 will show, even under the tariff of 1842, that the ad valorem duties produced 20 per cent. more than the specific duties. And how can it be otherwise in the absence of fraud? It may as well be said that a direct tax of one cent an acre on all lands, or five dollars on all houses, will produce as large a revenue as a tax in proportion to their values. In all cases of direct or indirect taxation, the tax, in proportion to value, incorporates itself proportionately with the price, and must, necessarily, increase the revenue.

And now, as to frauds: When there are but five or six duties, as under the tariff of 1846, and hundreds of different duties under the specific system, it is much easier to perpetrate frauds by changing names and classification of articles, than by reducing their values. That there were comparatively no frauds under the tariff of 1846, is proved by the immense augmentation of revenue; but still more by the favorable balance of our foreign trade, as compared with previous systems. Thus, with imports under the tariff of 1846, valued at the custom house at $350,000,000, if there had been an under valuation of only ten per cent., as compared with real values and consequent sales here, it would have turned the balance against the country, from that cause alone, $35,000,000 in gold a year. There is another insuperable objection to the specific system, viz.: that it unnecessarily and invariably taxes labor vastly more than capital, and the poor, in a much greater proportion than the rich, upon the goods consumed. Under the system of specific duties of so much per pound, or yard, or gallon, &c., the specific duty is the same. The rich, who purchase the costly article bearing only *the same specific* duty, pay, in proportion to value, less than one-half what is paid by the poor, who purchase a cheaper and less costly article. If we take all the costly articles purchased by the rich, bearing, under the present tariff, the same specific duty as the inferior article bought by the poor, we will find the difference against them exceeds $20,000,000 a year. Such is the immense additional tax exacted from labor under the system of specific duties. I know how fashionable it was to denounce the entire ad valorem system of 1846 as a novelty, but the experiment was completely successful, and the reason why it was a novelty was, that Europe is ruled by kings and oligarchies, that the laws are made by the wealthy few, and so framed as to exact the largest duty from labor and the least from capital. Switzerland, a republic, is with us on this question.

But the tariff of 1846, although it remained much longer in operation than any other tariff, and produced much more beneficial results, was susceptible of great improvements, especially in its application to the present condition of our country—

1st. The raw material of manufactures, as recommended in my first annual report, should be duty free, as is the practice of all enlightened nations. This proposition, then made by me, was to some extent defeated at that time by Mr. Calhoun. His argument was this—that, so far as no revenue was collected on the raw material of manufactures imported here, we must make good the loss from other articles, and that this was an unjust and unconstitutional discrimination in favor of American manufactures. My answer was—first, that it would never be unconstitutional to permit any one or more articles to come in duty free; second, that Mr. Calhoun had agreed to a large free list in the compromise tariff of 1832; third, that, in point of fact, there was no real loss of revenue, but an actual gain, resulting in this way: That, as our imports were measured by our exports, specie only liquidating occasional balances, and that, as we reduced our exports, we were necessarily diminishing our imports, and decreasing our revenue. To illustrate this, I said that dyestuffs are now free from duty, and we have a considerable export of dyed-goods to foreign countries. But if we impose a tax upon dyestuffs, which are admitted duty free by all other countries, we shall either annihilate or gradually diminish our exports of dyed goods, correspondingly decrease our imports, and diminish the revenue. This proved to be the case, as shown by the tables of our exports of dyed goods under the tariff of 1846, as compared with those of 1842. After a close investigation of this subject, and after examining the tariffs and the manufacturing establishments of foreign countries in 1851–2, and 1863–4, I am convinced, that, to admit the raw material of manufactures in all cases, duty free, would greatly increase our wealth, augment our exports, imports, and revenue, and diminish the burdens of taxation. Let us remember that, in taking the duty off the raw material, the consumers, the people of the United States, get the manufactured article at a lower rate. This, then, is another step in the reduction of taxes. With this principle in view, we could take up the five and ten per cent. schedules, and having admitted, duty free, all the articles specified in them, constituting the raw material of manufactures, we should abolish those two schedules, and put the remaining articles into the fifteen per cent. schedule, thus simplifying and improving the system and increasing the revenue.

2d. All the textile fabrics, and all mixtures of them, whether of wool, cotton, flax, hemp, silk, &c., should be placed in the thirty per cent. schedule. This would wonderfully simplify the system, prevent frauds, and largely increase the revenue, whilst, as an incidental aid to manufactures, so far as tariffs can help them at all, it would be beneficial.

3d. All wines, all malt and spirituous liquors, together with tobacco and its manufactures, should bear a duty equal to the excise, with an additional duty of fifty per cent. ad valorem.

4th. The duties on all other foreign luxuries consumed in this country should be increased to such a rate, as would, in every case, bring the largest amount of revenue.

5th. The duty on iron and all its manufactures should be 40 per cent. ad valorem, for two reasons: First, because it would only place them on an equality with manufactures of textile fabrics, when the raw material of manufactures should be duty free. Second, because this duty will bring more revenue than any other, and we now want all we can get from the tariff. It is a curious historical fact, that on a thorough investigation in 1846 of the duties which would bring the most revenue, I finally arrived at the conclusion that 40 per cent. on iron and its manufactures would bring more revenue than any other duty. On exhibiting these results at that day to a Southern Representative in Congress, and having convinced him of the truth of this position, he made, in the House of Representatives an offer to the iron interest of Pennsylvania and other States to place the duty on iron and all its manufactures at 40 per cent. ad valorem, if they would support the bill. This condition was necessary, because Mr. Calhoun had declared, that if these duties were placed at 40 per cent. ad valorem, he would oppose the measure. As the whole scheme would be defeated by Mr. Calhoun's opposition, if the iron interests would not unite with us, which they refused to do, the scheme was abandoned. But the fact still remains that a duty of 40 per cent. ad valorem on iron and all its manufactures would produce more revenue than any other rate. I regret very much to differ with my native State as regards coal. It is emphatically the great raw material of manufactures, of locomotion, and of steam power on the water and on the land, and, as fuel, is an absolute necessary of life. It will be remembered, that when the duties were changed, in the tariff of 1846, to an ad valorem duty of 30 per cent. on coal, Pennsylvania denounced the measure, and considered it destructive of her interests, especially as connected with Nova Scotia coal. But it produced no such results; and even after Nova Scotia coal became duty free, under our reciprocity treaties, our coal producers were not injured. On the contrary, the increase of coal mined from 1850 to 1860 was over 169 per cent. —namely, from 7,173,750 tons in 1850 to 19,365,765 tons in 1860. (See census table 13, page 173.) It is the success of all the great interests of the country, and especially of the great iron interest, creating such a vast demand for coal, that is infinitely more important than all duties upon the foreign product, and it seems to me that coal ought to be duty free.

With these and some minor changes in the system, developed by experience, and with the prevention of smuggling, growing out of reduced duties, it can be demonstrated that such a tariff would produce an annual revenue of at least two hundred millions of dollars a year, increasing at least six per cent. every year, being in a compound ratio of the augmentation of our wealth and population.

To obtain those results, however, we must first resume specie payments, restore the Union, re-establish the prosperity of the South, and abolish the whole system of internal taxation, except as hereinafter stated:

1. In addition to the taxes on the national banks now imposed by law, yielding, according to the last report, $8,000,000, I would impose but one *additional* tax upon them. It would be, that, whilst permitting them all to loan money at one uniform rate of seven per cent. per annum, as ought to have been done originally, they should pay over, annually, to the Government one-half their *net* profit realized during the year over seven per cent. I I think this would be fair to the Government, just to the banks, and satisfactory to the people, and would ultimately yield a very large revenue. As the present capital of the national banks is $425,000,000, and yields in all its operations $8,000,000 revenue to the nation, and as our bank capital, as shown by the census, doubles every ten years, this capital, at that rate of increase, would be $850,000,000 in 1878, $1,700,000,000 in 1888, and $3,400,000,000 in 1898. This would double the present tax every decade, and make it $64,000,000 in 1898. But if, under the additional tax proposed by me, the net annual profits should only by one per cent. exceed seven per cent. that tax would amount to $2,125,000 in 1868, $4,250,000 in 1878, $8,500,000 in 1888, and $17,000,000 in 1898. Thus, the banks in 1898 would pay a tax of $81,000,000, and soon more than liquidate the whole interest of our debt. This tax, too, would be collected without any expense or embarrassment.

To accomplish all this, our national bank system should no longer be a monopoly in the hands of the few, but all who will comply with the laws of Congress ought to be permitted to increase their capital or establish new institutions. That this would increase the currency of the country, is not denied. But, upon the resumption of specie payments, these banks could only be established upon a gold basis and upon actual capital, with the absolute security of their notes by deposits of United States stocks with the Government. Based upon such securities as these, banks, like bankers, would only increase according to the law of supply and demand, as they should do, and there would be no danger of any too great or too rapid augmentation, for the evil would correct itself by diminished business. This, however, should only be permitted on the resumption of specie payments, with specie reserves, in place of legal tenders, which would all have been paid in gold. On the resumption of specie payments, national banks would, of course, be established in California and all the gold-bearing States and Territories, because their paper would be equivalent to gold, and always redeemable upon demand. On the restoration of the Union and the renewed prosperity of the South, the number of banks would be largely increased there. Whilst all business, including bank circulation, has been permitted heretofore to increase, as it should, with the augmenting wealth of the country, it is a strange anomaly that bank capital and circulation alone should be limited to a fixed and arbitrary sum, although there is an increasing demand for more circulation.

Our bank capital from 1850 to 1860 increased, according to the census, nearly *one hundred* per cent. The aggregate capital of these national banks is now $425,000,000; but it would have been much greater but for the monopoly restrictions imposed by law. Suppose that under the free banking system the capital should double every ten years, it would, as we have seen, be $850,000.000 in 1878, $1,700,000,000 in 1888, and $3,400,000,000 in 1898, and, as we have seen, would soon absorb for circulation the whole debt of the country, and thus soon enable us to hold the whole national debt at home. But the greatest effect of all would be in sustaining the Government and perpetuating the Union, making us one nation so far as money is concerned. Then every bank which held our bonds, and every citizen of every State holding the money based upon them, would be virtually and directly interested in sustaining the Government and perpetuating the Union. Indeed, if this system had been in full operation in 1860, secession would have been impossible, because, by that act, the South would have destroyed all its own banks and moneyed resources, and because the State banks in the South were the very citadels of secession, supplying mainly the loans upon which the conflict was conducted there.

In the third edition of my London letters, in letter No. 5, page 24, and Appendix, page 3, it will be seen by the returns of the census that the gross product of our agriculture, manufactures, mines, and fisheries, was $5,290,000,000 in 1860. It was in fact greater, as there were many omissions in the census. It has been demonstrated in a recent letter of mine to the Commissioner of the General Land Office, prepared at his request, that, at this time, the amount of these products connected with *domestic* exchanges exceeds $5,000,000,000. It is estimated by political economists, that, from the first wholesale purchase, through the various changes, down to the sale to the actual consumer, these products are exchanged, on an average, four times. This would make the annual exchanges of these products equal to $20,000,000,000. But we have a great many other exchanges besides the sale of products, such as the enormous sums paid to railroads for freight and passengers, and for navigation on canals, rivers, lakes, and oceans; for rents, and interest, and insurance, &c., and all the various and multiplied business of life. In a nation having now thirty-seven millions of people, forty thousand miles of railroads, and at least twenty-five billions of wealth, as shown by the census, our total exchanges and re-exchanges must amount to thirty billions of dollars a year. We may begin to form some idea of the prodigious amount of these transactions, from the fact, that the amounts exchanged annually through the clearing-house by the banks of the city of New York alone, amounted in 1860 to over $7,000,000,000. Now, if the domestic exchanges throughout the whole country amount to $30,000,000,000 a year, a loss of one per cent. per annum would be $300,000,000 a year. Under our old State bank system, the loss on exchanges from the varying value of State paper in passing from State to State, and often from county to county, would certainly average at least one per cent. on the amounts of money exchanged. Charge this on only one-half the amount of our exchanges, and the annual tax imposed in that way upon the people of the United States, would reach one hundred and fifty millions of dollars. But this was not the only loss. During the sixty-four years of the operation of the State bank system, besides many partial and local suspensions and failures, there were eight general suspensions of specie payments, accompanied with great revulsions in business and incalculable losses. These losses did not merely affect the stockholders and depositors, but they impaired or destroyed the whole bank circulation held by the people. The depreciation would, perhaps, vary from ten to twenty per cent. during the suspension, but hundreds of banks would never resume, and their circulation become utterly worthless, or greatly depreciated in value. It is almost impossible even to make an approximate estimate to the vast losses sustained by the American people from the failure and suspension of State banks. Now, by the present national system, there can be no failure in the circulation, and the total losses in other ways, during their whole period of existence, has not reached one-fourth of one per cent. of their capital; and there may be, so far as the deposits are concerned, still further security. Indeed, nearly the whole loss arose from the want of a provision to prohibit disbursing officers to deposit with national banks, except with such as should have secured *all* Government deposits, by disbursing officers as well as by the Treasury, by United States stocks. I should consider, then, the destruction of the national banking system as an immense calamity to the country, to be accompanied, at this time, by a tremendous revulsion, and forcing hundreds of millions of our bonds upon the already overburdened markets of Europe and America But, it is proposed by some, to call in the national bank currency of three hundred millions of dollars, substituting therefor an equal amount of legal tenders. We shall then have nearly seven hundred millions of legal tenders, and no national bank currency. Now, in the first place, these three hundred millions of national bank currency, rest upon an *actual* capital of three hundred and forty millions vested in bonds of the Government, deposited in the United States Treasury. They rest, besides, on all the capital and reserves of the bank and fixed liability of the shareholders; but upon what would the seven hundred millions of legal tenders rest? Upon nothing but the faith of the Government. There would be no bonds in which they could be funded, nor any period fixed for redemption, and bearing no interest, and with no guaranty against further expansion. The seven hundred millions of legal tenders and national bank notes are worth now $500,000,000 in gold. What would these seven hundred millions of legal tenders be worth when the Government had cut loose from the banks and put its own paper mill in exclusive operation? They certainly would not command fifty cents on the dollar in gold, and this, therefore, would be equivalent to an actual contraction of the currency of thirty per cent., or $150,000,000, by releasing the reserves now required to be kept in the vaults of the banks. And yet the Government and the people would lose by the depreciation of all the bonds and legal tenders held by them, the Government expenditures would enormously increase by payments in depreciated paper, and the interest gained on the amount released from their legal tender reserves by the banks, would be greatly less than the tax now actually paid by the banks to the nation. The expansionists would gain nothing, for, the depreciation of the currency would make the increased volume worth less than the smaller circulation was before. The only way to expand safely and beneficially to the Government and the people, is by a foreign loan, to substitute gold for greenbacks, and increase the number of national banks by repealing the monopoly and restrictive clauses.

How are the transfers of the Government to be made, and at what expense and risk, when the national banks shall have been abolished and their circulation withdrawn? Who, then, are to be the fiscal agents of the Government, and where, with whom, and how are its receipts to be deposited, for the assistant treasurers deal only in gold? Is this issue of $700,000,000 of legal tenders what is desired by expansionists? If so, how long is this paper carnival of the treasury to last, and when, or how, are we to resume specie payments? Why, specie payments could then only be resumed by a loan, if it could be obtained, or by gradual contraction, and what then would be the condition of the country? Why, the national bank circulation having disappeared, legal tenders would have been exhausted, and we should be left without any paper circulation whatever. Or is it intended that this shall be a permanent system when we shall have resumed specie payments? If so, is the Government to turn banker, and how, and where, and in what manner, and at what places, is it to redeem from day to day its treasury notes in specie, and how, and by whom, are they to be reissued? The national bank notes are redeemable in the various towns and cities throughout the Union, but such an arrangement could never be made by the Government to redeem its notes throughout the country, without gigantic frauds and stupendous losses. Suppose the Government would keep two or three hundred millions of dollars in specie *here* to redeem seven hundred millions of legal tenders, what becomes of the man in New York holding these legal tenders, desiring the specie every day and every hour to meet contingencies and the wants of business. What are the men to do who would require it in all the Western cities, more and more remote from the seat of Government, especially in San Francisco? The merchants there, say in a given day, want two or three millions of dollars in gold for remittance to China, or Japan, or Mexico, or Central or Southern America. They hold legal tenders, but how are they to get the gold? It is obvious that these notes would be gradually depreciating, and that, as a consequence, the specie at the seat of Government would soon all be drawn out. And if the Government had not specie to meet all the notes, it must fail and be protested. Is the Government prepared to keep $700,000,000 in gold to meet, at various points, the demand for gold, subject to all the risks of fraud and peculation, or is it to keep up forever an irredeemable and depreciated paper currency? The whole idea of Government paper, as a permanent system of circulation, has uniformly failed wherever it has been tried, and has always either been abandoned, or has reduced the Government to bankruptcy. When the Government issues at its pleasure the whole currency of the country in paper, the temptation to over-issue, and increase expenses, is irresistible; suspension follows; the depreciation goes on, augmenting from day to day, until repudiation finally winds up the drama of ruin and disgrace. There may be some of the national banks that would gladly present their notes and withdraw their bonds from the Treasury, circulating legal tender notes, escaping considerable taxation, and realizing increased profits at the expense of the people. But *there is not one of them* that would not know what would be the necessary termination of the system, and would prepare in time to guard against the catastrophe. Let us go on and perfect and improve, but not destroy our national banking system. If further checks are wanted that would not impair the system, let them be made. If further reserves of specie are necessary upon resumption, let them be required. If the whole of their deposits, as well as of their circulation, can be secured by national bonds, let this be provided for also. If, as is easy, a fair and equitable arrangement can be made by which the country banks would redeem their notes, not only at their own counters but at the city of New York, like the old Suffolk bank system of New England, let that be done, with proper aids and facilities from the Government, so as to prevent loss or expense to the New York city banks or the country banks.

When Secretary of the Treasury, I urged earnestly upon Congress the granting of authority for the proper steps to be taken to decimalize our weights and measures, and to produce, as far as practicable, uniformity in them, and an international coinage of uniform value throughout the world. Congress has now taken a great and glorious first step toward a decimal system of weights and measures, and I believe it is now in its power to hasten the establishment of international coins of similar value throughout the world. If we would make the French franc a unit, rising or falling with the larger or smaller coins, making half eagles equal to twenty-five French francs, so marked upon it, as proposed by me in 1851, and our dollar equal to five francs, with a national bank currency perfectly secured, redeemable with absolute certainty in gold, at the counter of the bank, as also at New York city, and payable in a gold currency of an established and uniform value throughout the world, I believe our bank notes would eventually obtain a large circulation in Europe, permeate all North and South America, and, crossing the Pacific, reach China and Japan, and be received as our United States bank notes once were there. Such a system would greatly accelerate the period when this country, through its commercial emporium, would become the centre of the commerce and exchanges of the world. At present, our exchanges on London, usually quoted at from 9 to 10 per cent., are a mystery to the great masses of the people, they not recognizing the difference between the parliamentary and congressional value of the pound sterling. At present, exchange from Europe on this country has no fixed value, and is always obtained at great loss, whilst in Asia and Egypt, such a thing as exchange on this country is hardly recognized.

I now pass from the bank question to the last topic, viz: Internal taxation.

Almost everything is taxed now, either by a stamp tax, an income tax, a tax on sales, or an excise on nearly every article that is consumed by the people; and an army of tax-gatherers are employed, at a vast expense, accompanied by enormous frauds, to collect a small portion of this tax. Now, I would disband nearly this whole legion of tax collectors and assessors, and repeal the whole system of internal taxation, except the excise on wines, malt and spiritous liquors, and tobacco. I am confident that under such a system at least one hundred and thirty millions of dollars a year, in gold, or its equivalent, could be collected from these articles. By table 21 of the census of 1860, the number of gallons of spirituous liquors distilled during the year ending June 1, 1860, exceeded eighty-eight millions of dollars. I am opposed to any reduction of the excise on whiskey, believing it to be one of those articles, above all others, from which we ought to collect the largest possible revenue; and confident, by the experience of England for years in collecting a tobacco tax, where a much larger proportional rate was assessed and collected, that the present whiskey tax can be realized. Surely we ought not to surrender this tax to fraud and villany without still further efforts for its collection. If all these results are realized, the revenue would amount to $340,000,000 a year in gold, which leaves a margin of nearly one hundred millions per annum above what would be required to carry on the Government, and pay the interest and a small proportion of the principal of our public debt.

Should this system yield a large surplus, as I believe it would, I would still further reduce taxation in the following manner:

1st. By admitting duty free coffee, tea, and sugar, which have become great necessaries of life in this country.

2d. If there were still a considerable surplus revenue, I would take the duty from other necessaries of life not produced at home.

3d. If a surplus still remained, I would devote it to such great works of national internal improvement as the ship canals to the West, which, in augmented wealth, would fourfold repay the expenditures.

Our present system of taxation is the most onerous ever imposed upon any people, and is utterly destructive of the prosperity of our country.

Our present tariff is also most unequal, oppressive, and unjust. It is grievously onerous upon agriculture, commerce, navigation, shipbuilding, the mines and fisheries, whilst even manufactures, in connection with our present wretched excise system, are languishing under its inflictions. The present tariff, besides the tax of $150,000,000 a year upon imports, the duties on which are paid by the people into the Treasury in gold, exacts another tax of at least $350,000,000 a year in the enhanced prices of rival protected domestic articles. This can be readily proved by comparing the prices current in gold of such domestic articles with the prices of similar articles produced in other countries. Thus, the tariff taxes the people of the United States to the extent of $500,000,000 a year, of which only $150,000,000 goes into the Treasury, and the remaining $350,000,000 go into the pockets of the protected classes. And yet, even they are not prosperous, on account of the diminished demand for their products, and because they are also burdened, with the rest of the people, by the weight of intolerable taxation.

The annual taxes now paid by our people as the result of the tariff, we have seen, are at least $500,000,000 a year. Add to this another $500,000,000 a year as the result, directly and indirectly, of our internal system of taxation, including the stupendous and atrocious whiskey and other frauds, and our national taxation, in time of profound peace, amounts to $1,000,000,000 a year. Less than half of this goes into the Treasury. This is independent of State, county, city, and municipal taxation, which is enormous. This billion of dollars a year, as the census shows, is about one-seventh of the gross values of our present annual products, and can be borne by no people on earth. Repudiation is the necessary result of the continuance of such a system.

Since my return from Europe, I have conversed on this snbject with many intelligent persons, including leading manufacturers of iron, wool, and cotton, and I have not yet met a single individual who does not agree with me that the tariff, as above proposed, together with the changes as regards internal taxation, would be far better for them than the present system. What will be said of this by political manufacturers, I do not know.

If we look at the effect of repudiation upon the morals of the people, and upon State, municipal, and individual contracts, the result must be disastrous. When an individual able to pay refuses to do so, he is justly considered a fraudulent bankrupt, and the law looks upon him as such. In morals, there is no difference between a nation able to pay and refusing and an individual. There may be no human law under which nations violating their just obligations can be punished, but they cannot escape with impunity. Besides the disastrous results on their material interests, such nations justly become outcasts among communities; and, in the providence of God, sooner or later, meet with just retribution. It is a part of the Divine law, applicable as well to nations as to individuals, that injustice carries with it retributive punishment, and history, sacred and profane, abounds with such examples. Franklin's maxim, endorsed by Washington, that "honesty is the best policy," is as true of communities as of individuals.

On this great question which now attracts the attention of our country and the world, Congress, and every member must make a record that will be read and studied now and in all succeeding ages. There will be a roll of honor and of shame, on which will be inscribed names never to be obliterated. There is nothing so enduring as truth. It may be crushed for the moment, but eventually is sure to triumph. To say that any gigantic national crime, such as repudiation, will not meet the retributive justice of Heaven, is to believe that God has abdicated the moral government of the universe.

Although the toiling millions may have little of this world's goods to leave behind them, yet, in life, all can strive to maintain, and in death to transmit to our children, the priceless heritage of a nation's honor. It is the joint inheritance of every American. Who can estimate its value? Better than gold, dearer than life, as well may we strive to number the stars that are lost in the shadowy verges of receding space, or count the years and centuries that roll on forever and ever, in *secula, seculorum*. If God has given us great wealth and power and priceless freedom; if He has endowed us with the advancing, peaceful possession of a continent stretching from pole to pole and from sea to sea, He will surely exact from us the performance of corresponding duties. First among these, are the maintenance of honor and the preservation of good faith. Be just and fear not. Let us be just, and no imagination can conceive the fulfilling realties and advancing glories of the great Republic.

It may be well that this technical objection has been thrown in our way to swerve us from the path of duty. We were tempted, but we fell not. Let the American Congress proclaim that our faith shall be preserved, when our credit wil rise higher and higher, emigration will come, and capital and labor, and money where they are most safe; and gold will pour in upon us in Pactolean streams, and long before the close of this century, our debt will scarcely be counted as a fractional per cent. in writing up the ledger of the nation's wealth and resources.

R. J. WALKER.

www.ingramcontent.com/pod-product-compliance
Lightning Source LLC
LaVergne TN
LVHW020641110826
845149LV00004B/1313

* 9 7 8 1 4 1 8 1 9 0 3 0 9 *